BREAKUPS, BREAKDOWNS, AND J.R.R. TOLKIEN'S THE LORD OF THE RINGS

A COLLECTION OF POEMS FROM SOMEONE WHO HASN'T WRITTEN POEMS BEFORE

Ian Saad

BookLeaf Publishing
India | USA | UK

Breakups, Breakdowns, and J.R.R. Tolkien's The Lord of The
Rings

A collection of poems from someone who hasn't written
poems before

© 2021 Ian Saad

Presentation by *BookLeaf Publishing*

Web: www.bookleafpub.com

E-mail: info@bookleafpub.com

ISBN: 9789358360875

First edition 2021

Crockpot

To the Ian who grew up in America because his parents moved to this country just before he was born

To the Ian who grew up surrounded by cousins. And made movies and took art class with his cousins.

To the Ian who was terrified of his sister

To the Ian that played super smash bros for the 1st time at his friend Brian's house

To the Ian that biked around the neighborhood

To you.. I am sorry

To the Ian who didn't answer when asked what team Barry Bonds played for, not because he didn't know the answer but because he was too afraid to get it wrong

To the Ian who wanted to be a cartoonist

To the Ian who made comic books

To the Ian who broke his front teeth falling face

first on concrete playing wall ball

To the Ian who almost drowned in the ocean

To the Ian who bullied that kid that everyone

bullied

To the Ian who had his first kiss to a boy

To you.. I am sorry

To the Ian who wore purple pants

To the Ian who had a giant afro

To the Ian that played the saxophone

To the Ian who chose Jazz band over ceramics

and always wondered "what if?"

To the Ian who wrecked his car listening to the

guitar solo of Freebird.. On April 1st

To the Ian who played football

To the Ian who was terrified of football

To the Ian that finally got it and put in all he had

To the Ian who was Alpha male of the month in

the Daily Urinal.. A school newspaper for the

men's bathroom

To the Ian who became good friends with that
kid that everyone bullied.
To the Ian who played a lot of World of
Warcraft
To the Ian who met a flower
To the Ian that loved that flower so hard
To the Ian who held that flower for 5 years
To you.. I am sorry

To the Ian who was so excited to have a
roommate in college
To the Ian that found truly funny people
To the Ian that laughed so much
To the Ian who said nothing on the phone when
his parents told him they were getting divorced
To the Ian who bounced around major after
major
To the Ian who took every sculpture class the
school had to offer
To the Ian who wishes he did more
To the Ian who played a lot of Starcraft

To the Ian that really saw people and wanted
so desperately to be seen
To the Ian that misses the rain
To you.. I am sorry

To the Ian who worked some pretty weird jobs
To the Ian that plays the didgeridoo
To the Ian who cracks under pressure
To the Ian who fell in love at the wild animal
park
To the Ian who learned about real love
To the Ian that loves everyone
To the Ian who loves coffee
To the Ian that loves Super Smash Bros. Melee
for the Nintendo Gamecube
To the Ian who felt his soul being crushed
commuting through traffic
To the Ian who felt
To you.. I am sorry

To the Ian that opened up more than he ever
thought he would

To the Ian that can glow

To the Ian who's glow captured the eye of a
sloth

To the Ian that was loved by that sloth

To the Ian that was taken to great places
because of that sloth

To the Ian that wouldn't be who he is if he
hadn't met that sloth

To the Ian that didn't deserve that sloth

To the Ian that deserved that sloth

To you.. I am sorry

To the Ian that climbs rocks

And sings in the car

And loves puns

And makes animal noises

And works for an actually good company with
actually good people

And is being a better friend

And isn't getting old

And finally understands

To all the Ians…

Thank you.

I am so, so sorry for everything that's

happened

And for getting in your way

And stopping you from everything you could

have done

But I hope you know..

That everything that's cooked in a crock pot

comes out oh so juicy

Petrified Words

I waited in a whole foods parking lot

Breathing out the lingering words

From the night before

Breathing out that tension left

By those stuck words

Today I read the petrified words

Of writers past

I climbed the mountain hollow

As I dug deep and learned from those before
me

With the wind in my face

And my hands on the earth

My eyes open up and wake

As I breathe out the last

Of those petrified words.

Hobbit

I want to take this ring to mordor
I want to throw it into the flames within
and never look back..
But I cannot.

For you see I am just a hobbit
Merrily strolling through fields
Waking up outside in the sunshine
With a belly full
Of laughter shared
I may be small but I
Move the earth with my feet alone
Stepping ever louder
Echoing a great weight

We Hobbits must burden the weight of our
rings
Their Power pulling us down
Holding us down.

Catching our gaze

Keeping our gaze.

Calling us in

As we call to it

But no this precious I cannot burn

On the mountaintops

For she carries me.

How would I find mordor

If not for her

How would I hide from dragons

How could I live so rich and so long

Without her at my side

How could I meet friends all over

How could I stand being alone

Without her in my hands

No… no I shall not follow Frodo's footsteps

Up to mordor's peak.

No I will not hunch like smeagle

Crippled forevermore.

I will follow Bilbo's path

There and back again.

Cabinet

A cabinet in the sky waits to be built

And calls to be woken from its slumber.

All the doors, and the shelves, and knobs

Those I carry, I carry those pieces once built

To the top of the ladder.

To make the cabinet be.

A cabinet in the sky waits to be filled

With knickknacks and trinkets from past lives.

They sit united, preserved, reflecting light

That shines behind them

In the empty box once built.

Floating at the end of the ladder.

A cabinet in the sky waits to be seen.

Its curiosities marveled by travelers and

guests.

Their faces, their spirits, lifted

As the cabinet longs to be.

Yes I'll stand atop the ladder
Once the ladder has been built.

A cabinet in the sky will be taken down.
As all things that are up ought to.
Once built, once assembled, once carried
The cabinet rests as whole.
For in the sky the cabinet shall slumber
Waiting for it to come to be.

When a Force Lifts

When a force lifts we feel light

And free to soar as we take flight

From fettered to feathered our body ignites

And carries itself to new heights

Beyond what it knew before

Fear when a force lifts

For what it held down might drift

Away and disperse. An unknown gift

Now gone. Without it will we rift

Apart, leaving what we knew before

Two forces now repel from ground

stood on. A magnetic bond turned around

by a new force that holds us down

How terrible to feel flight, only to be bound.

If Icarus could fly why can't I

As we both knew before

A Breath Escapes

A breath escapes and becomes the wind

Becoming far greater than it was before.

It thrusts itself with heat

It crashes into the earth

And moves the oceans like no one could.

Breathe in.

Breathe out.

A breath escapes and becomes the wind

Lifting birds and carrying sound

For our ears and our eyes to witness.

We recognize not one, not one

Only the wind.

Breathe in.

Breathe out.

A breath escapes and becomes the wind

Rushing through your hair

Forcing your eyes shut tight

As it swirls and dances

Rejoicing to be united again

Breathe in.

The wind is pulled apart

And drawn inward.

A small piece fills your lungs.

Cleaved the wind gives you energy

Making you as the wind.

Making you the wind.

Yet a calmness overtakes you as you quiet

The parts once divided

With a gust of stillness

With a stillness as the wind.

Be still as the wind as you

Breathe out.

A breath escapes and becomes the wind

Just Fit

Like peanut butter and jelly

Like socks and shoes

Like salt and pepper

And cereal with milk

Like me and you

And two puzzle pieces

With bent corners

And matching patterns

That look like they line up

Like all things that just fit

Together they sum greater than their parts

To take each other to greater heights.

Until they can't.

To move forward

Some pieces have to be taken apart

To be a part of the greater puzzle

A picture that two little pieces simply can't

comprehend.

Good Enough

In the mornings I feel good enough
As I convince myself to get up
And out and begin the day.

At noon I feel good enough
As I avoid some task with some food
And eat a sandwich

In the evenings I feel good enough
Ready to fall
And to rise the next day having slept good
enough

Sometimes I feel good enough
Sometimes not so good, but enough
Of that. Is there enough good
In the good feelings?
Is there enough bad
In the bad?

Enough goodness together must be good

enough

To fill our satisfaction. But is being satisfied

good enough

When we want more than good enough?

Am I good enough?

The things I do I'm certainly not good enough

At. But enough of this.

Maybe instead I'm bad

Or perhaps just enough.

Enough can only be good enough

If it is good.

And bad enough isn't a thing

Itch

It started with an itch

A tingling feeling we can't ignore

Even when we do

It started with an itch

On my shoulder

On the left side

Am I supposed to shoulder

What's left after you

And I did we what we did?

Tension held and a

Posture adapted to

Hide.

Hide from what's left of you and I

It started with an itch

Just on the corner of my mouth

Slowly it spread to the jaw

It spread so slowly I didn't know

I didn't know what it would mean

Once that itch was gone.

What words I could speak

How clearly I can sound

Without that itch holding my mouth down

It started with an itch

On my feet

Both feet

In different ways

She gave them hope

That they could move

And wiggle free from this itch

With time and attention

And care

These feet could fill shoes

I needed to fill

And break free from those shoes

That I didn't

It always starts with an itch

Something telling you to pay attention

And look and listen and explore

Without an itch we can't know

What needs attention

And how to fix what lies broken

Under that tingling feeling we can't ignore

Don't ignore and don't scratch

Transition

We each handle transitions differently.

Some nervous, some flourish

In those moments between moments.

They check inward

They recenter and adjust

Before they return to the moments

Around those moments.

But I, I live in that in-between

And see them all.

Their hidden truths shown through

Those doors ajar and open blinds.

But with eyes open blind I miss the house.

The house and its foundation.

The neighborhood, the streets.

I'm lost in the city

Mesmerized by what I see in-between.

The River Runs By The Land

The fish know the bull

For who she is

Strong and gentle

And led astray.

The fish can see where the is bull is headed

For the river runs by the land.

But the fish cannot reach the bull

For she is too far and

Knows not the fish.

The fish are loving and calm

And want to guide the bull

On her path led astray.

The river runs by the land

But not through it.

The fish can only glimpse the bull

On the bridge now built across the river.

The bull chooses to not see

The fish for she knows not the fish

As she once did.

But she knows on the land

The fish cannot walk.

The fish have resolved to let the bull walk

Walk as she will always walk

As she always has walked.

For she is not led she leads

Her way astray from the fish

The fish who long

For her return to the riverside

Even for just a moment

Hard Decisions

When a decision must be made

We learn that

We are not one person

We are several.

We are several mixed together

That take turns

Being heard.

And only one should hold the wheel

When we reach a fork in the road

Which you will you be when you

Want to go

When you want

To grow

When you want

To create

When you want

Balance

When you want

A chance

To finally be heard

By the other yous.

The you that is heard is the you

That listens.

The you you are is not one person

You are several.

You are several mixed together

That take turns

Being heard.

So listen you

To the you you are

And the you want to become

It's never too late

To make a decision.

Cannot

Today I cannot

Provide a poem

For I am tired

And lazy

And actually sick

Do not judge me

For I am like you

And both of us don't want to write a poem

today

Suppression

We press down ourselves and our desires,
suppression
Others suppress our ideas and actions,
oppression
To suppress and oppress leaves a lasting
impression
On us today.

We doubt ourselves every moment, second
guessing
Others look at us passing judgement, they be
messing
To guess and mess with this mind this blessing
Is a curse today.

We see ourselves the only way we can,
reflected
Others see our image through their own lens,
infected

To shed a light on this may help it be corrected

If only for today

But no, not today

The Path Part 1

Sometimes the right time is the worst time.

Sometimes we are not who we are until those moments.

Those moments that set the path in motion.

Those moments that also put us on the path.

And those moments where we take steps.

Like the sloth you are we took our time.

Smelling flowers with hands tied behind our backs

Trekking to heights two sloths shouldn't be able.

In the forest we stood before a great tree

And as much as we wanted to

We could not climb together.

Sometimes the right time is the worst time.

I climbed the tree slow and steady

As you watched from below.

You watched with eyes full of excitement and fear and love

Unlike the rest of the world who was

Offended by a sloth climbing such a tree.

Looking down from the treetops I knew.

I knew I wasn't a sloth

I thought I could be

I wanted to be

But you knew all along

That there is never a right time to blaze a trail

forward

Sometimes the right time is the worst time.

The Path Part 2

Sometimes the right time is the worst time

Our opportunities come when we need them to

If we are ready we can take them

If we can't take them then we aren't ready

You came when I was ready

I saw both paths in front of me

And who I would be along each

I could no longer see the trees

Or the boxes I left behind

But the box I brought was open and sturdy

Thanks to you

Thanks to me

This time, this time I went off on my own

And went forward

Sometimes the right time is the worst time

The Path Part 3

Sometimes the right time is the worst time

We all see who walks where

On trails

On the hillside

By the ocean

In the river

Over rocks and standing over cliffs

But not on trees.

We need two hands to climb

And I have this box

And now the box is filled

Filled with memories and the weight of the past

So carefully I put the box down

For just a moment.

What harm could be done?

For I know this box of mine

And how sturdy it can be

Sometimes the right time is the worst time

From the treetops I see more

Than I could before

I see birds above and travelers all over

I see trail runners and photographers

I see paths I would not have found otherwise

Looking down I saw no one

I saw only the box

I saw it open and empty

It was the right time

It was the right time to climb and the worst time

to put down a box

But sometimes the right time is the worst time

Rest now

Rest now little fish

Return to the coral

That bright fading coral

Where the two of you can swim

And dance with each other

Seeing what the rest do not.

Rest now little fish

For you two are too much for the land

And the land is harsh and dry.

Rest now in calm waters

Rest as the company of two

Fogged Glasses

I stood there with fogged glasses

Not knowing whether to take them off

And clean them to clear the veil in front of me

Or to wait for the fog to spread thin and

For the world to reveal itself as it always does

I feel heat

Heat swirls off of me and hits the cold glass

While each breath slows it down

The fog keeps coming

In and out

It gradually gives way

It gradually gives way to the world behind

A natural rhythm I don't want to interrupt

But then again I could

I could simply take off the glass

And wipe clean the mist

That sits in my way.

I could remove this obstacle at any moment

I could easily take off the cold glass

At the cost of a sudden and brief blindness

I could clean the fog

That muddles my vision

Only at the cost of blindness

Of the world rushing in

Either way, clarity will come

I stood there with fogged glasses

Not knowing whether to take them off

And clean them to clear the veil in front of me

Or to wait for the fog to spread thin and

For the world to reveal itself as it always does.

They feel cold

How are they so cold.

They sit in front of me always

Working nonstop

As they bend light into my eyes

In just the right way.

How are they so cold

With all that movement

With everything passing

Through them

As they sit still

The world comes to them not me

I do not know the world

Am I afraid to take them off?

Afraid to see into this unknown

Afraid to see what I cannot see

What the world cannot show me.

Just because I know what's there

Doesn't mean I know what it feels like

I want to know what it feels like

So I stood there

I stood there with fogged glasses

Not knowing whether to take them off

And clean them to clear the veil in front of me

Or to wait for the fog to spread thin and

For the world to reveal itself as it always does.

Diver

Why do I do the things I do?

Why do I want the things I want?

Why do I like what I like?

Why do I dislike what I dislike?

I want to I dive free

Free from all that baggage

Everything they need to breathe underwater

And see underwater

And protect me from the harsh depths

There are those who do so free

Relaxed, yes relaxed even under the weight

and the pressure of the oceans deep

They can swim far and free

And be one with the life there

Unlike the diver

Safe and protected

But I should not shame the diver

For she is out there, out in the depths

While I am at the surface

Longing to swim

Where's Waldo

Where is Waldo?

When we look for Waldo we look all over

Behind the man on mars

Next to the protestor

On the cliff by the beach

When we look for Waldo we look all over

Somewhere between that club

And the hardware store

When I look I don't think

Eyes dart from corner to corner and

Around every shape and color

No rhyme or reason just by feel

And intuition Waldo comes to me

When you look you have to think

Every decision planned and optimal

Every rock turned over but

Never twice

You can't waste energy looking twice

And Waldo only hides in one place

We both met Waldo at the same time

Both excited at the result

Realizing our flaws in ourselves

And in each other

Both doubtful yet at the same time both so sure

In our own way to Waldo

Didn't expect to find

I didn't expect to find you there
   no, that was never the plan
I could have thought to find you there
   if my mind was open
I couldn't have thought you'd find me here
   where it all began
But I did expect to find some here
   once it was broken

I didn't expect to find me
   where you used to be

You used to be there

Dragon's Mouth

His wings steady still

His eyes piercingly sharp

Maybe he will take off

With the slightest irritation

And return to the mountains

That reach the skies above

But the dragon is but a statue

An idol, figured in place

Perfectly still, poised

Small and limited

Yet still the incense burns

And still the ash falls down

Onto the floor

Just missing the plate

And the dragon smirks

Reminder

Freshly roasted coffee

Locked tight in a jar

Locked tight to preserve

The aromatics and the flavors

Trapped within the beans

But we had to break the seal

Just for a moment

Just for a moment, each morning

Just the right amount removed

Now you keep the water warm

While you weigh the beans

And dial in the grind

Something once done for you

You now do for others

And you do what you do

As a lingering feeling swirls through the air

As that morning coffee dances

And reaches those around you

Some say that smell is most closely tied to

memory

Is this what's left?

Lingering memories

In the actions left behind?

A piece of me left in every part of you

Only to rise up and bloom

Just for a moment, each morning

Right now

What does this moment feel like?

Right now

Not then

No not then when you remember

But this moment

Right now.

What does this moment feel like

Before you put words to it?

Tell me

Traveling

As the sun sets over the mountains high

As the frogs speak up

I look across a land that I

That I would call vast

Unlike those that speak

Those that speak what I see.

As the mountains light up with the setting sun

As the stars reveal themselves in the sky once
blue

I think of travels once traveled

By we

But we can no longer see

What I see

There is so much

For I to see without we

Lucky

Lucky

Like two harmonicas

Scattered over the road

Lucky

Like sliding down a rock and

Jumping off just so

To not tumble down

Lucky

Like a happy dog

Brought up mountains

And through forests

Into lakes

With great people

Lucky to be me

Lucky to be here

Lucky to be

Lucky

The Valley

The valley calls to us

With a surreal, familiar voice

We know this voice

We've heard it before

Not sure where

We know we cannot hear it from afar

There's too much noise

Too much interference and static

But not here

Here we can hear it loud and clear

We can hear the voice of the valley

Echoing in the path once took by frozen giants

We can see how the earth is no different

Than the clay we played with

We see the death and life and beauty in both

We see time and scale and everything we are
not

Everything we cannot hear

When not here

The valley calls us, and we answer

I'm here

51

Dinner with a silent smile

Dinner with a silent smile

Is what I'm used to

No sharing No minimal conversation No tv on

Let's just all gather and sit a while

Even just us two

Let's eat dry overcooked meat in silence

Honestly it's pretty nice with less

Words

When we sit around

Feeling the air around

Watching our dogs go around

Doing their dogly things

And honestly it's pretty nice with less

Words

We have to make up

I don't think there's time to make up

All the things we could have said

At those dinners

So yes

Let's eat dry overcooked meat in silence

Just one more day

What's one more day?

Ignored

Why didn't we finish the Lord of The Rings?

I wanted to know

I wanted to know what happened to those

hobbits

And the mountains

What happened to Frodo, to Sam, Danny and

Kaniki

I thought sequels came one after another

Why did you fly away

And why did you come back?

Was it that dinosaur

Staring from the window?

Or the family you also

Didn't really have over there?

I'm here now, it's okay

Why did we stop playing?

Why did you stay in your room?

Is it because the bathtub was always

One drop away

From flooding the house?

It's just water after all

A cut only scars when

Not cared for in the right way.

So let's tend to the scars

Let's open up those wounds

So they can heal again

And be free from this pain once ignored

The boy who scoots

Before we learn to run we must all learn to walk

But what if we didn't have to walk

What if we could scoot?

What if we could slide on the ground

Using all fours?

Faster than any kid who walked!

He said

Not realizing what was set in motion

A boy who scoots in every way

Who finds his own solutions

Based on his own problems

Caused by scooting

Never knowing the right way

Or if there is a right way

Or if his way is wrong

But hey

Faster than any kid who walked!

He said

Not realizing what was set in motion

A boy who scoots in every way

Perhaps a boy made to scoot

Could never really walk as they do

Now a man that boy looks around

He looks at all those who walk

And all those that run

Are they happy?

Do they even know how they move

Or are they just moving

From A to B

What if we all stopped

What if we were all fast and free

And didn't care what we looked like

When we scooted from A to B